PICTI

SRA Specific Skill Series
for Reading

Identifying
Fact & Opinion

Sixth Edition

Columbus, OH

The **McGraw·Hill** Companies

SRAonline.com

 SRA

Send all inquiries to:
SRA/McGraw-Hill
8787 Orion Place
Columbus, OH 43240-4027

ISBN 0-07-604093-3

1 2 3 4 5 6 7 8 9 BCH 12 11 10 09 08 07 06 05

PURPOSE:

IDENTIFYING FACT AND OPINION is designed to help develop the important skill of understanding and recognizing the difference between facts and opinions. **IDENTIFYING FACT AND OPINION** requires students to analyze information and determine whether it can be researched and proved or if it is a feeling or belief.

FOR WHOM:

The skill **IDENTIFYING FACT AND OPINION** is developed through a series of books spanning ten levels (Picture, Preparatory, A, B, C, D, E, F, G, H,). The Picture Level is for students who have not acquired a basic sight vocabulary. The Preparatory Level is for students who have a basic sight vocabulary but are not yet ready for the first-grade-level book. Books A through H are appropriate for students who can read on levels one through eight, respectively.

THE NEW EDITION:

The sixth edition of the *Specific Skill Series for Reading* maintains the quality and focus that has distinguished this program for more than 40 years. A key element central to the program's success has been the unique nature of the reading selections. Fiction and nonfiction pieces about current topics have been designed to stimulate the interest of students, motivating them to use the comprehension strategies they have learned to further their reading. To keep this important aspect of the program intact, a percentage of the reading selections has been replaced in order to ensure the continued relevance of the subject material.

In addition, a significant percentage of the artwork in the program has been replaced to give the books a contemporary look. The cover photographs are designed to appeal to readers of all ages.

SESSIONS:

Short practice sessions are the most effective. It is desirable to have a practice session every day or every other day, using a few units in each session.

SCORING:

Students should record their answers on the reproducible worksheets. The worksheets make scoring easier and provide uniform records of the students' work. Using worksheets also avoids consuming the exercise books.

It is important for students to know how well they are doing. For this reason, units should be scored as soon as they have been completed. Then a discussion can be held in which students justify their choices. (The *Language Activity Pages,* many of which are open-ended, do not lend themselves to an objective score; thus there are no answer keys for these pages.)

GENERAL INFORMATION ON *IDENTIFYING FACT AND OPINION:*

IDENTIFYING FACT AND OPINION varies in content. It contains fiction and nonfiction stories that will stretch the imagination, spark interest in new areas, promote admiration for outstanding achievements, and develop a sense of wonder about our world.

There is only one correct answer for each question. Students practice identifying facts and opinions they read in the story or see in the picture. **IDENTIFYING FACT AND OPINION** means recognizing which statements can be proven and which are feelings or beliefs.

SUGGESTED STEPS:

1. Students read the story. (In the Picture Level books, the students look at the pictures. In the Prep Level books, the students look at the pictures and listen to the stories.)

2. After completing the story, students answer the questions and choose the letter of the correct answer.

3. Students write the letters of the correct answers on the worksheets.

4. Students may refer back to the pictures and stories before choosing an answer.

RELATED MATERIALS:

Specific Skill Series Assessment Book provides the teacher with a pretest and posttest for each skill at each grade level. These tests will help the teacher assess the students' performance in each of the nine comprehension skills.

A **fact** is something that is true. You can check a fact to make sure that it is true. These are facts:

> Oranges grow on trees.
> Horses have four legs.

An **opinion** is a feeling, idea, or belief. You cannot check to see if an opinion is true or false. These are opinions:

> Fall is the most beautiful time of the year.
> Snowboarding is really exciting.

You can look for facts and opinions as you read. You can look for facts in pictures too. A picture of a girl throwing a ball for a dog contains these facts:

> There is one girl and one dog in the picture.
> The girl and the dog are playing with a ball.

There are 50 units in this book. For each unit, think about the pictures carefully. Then answer the questions about the pictures.

The traffic light is red.

Is this a fact or an opinion?

(**A**) Fact or (**B**) Opinion

Riding the bus is fun.

Is this a fact or an opinion?

(A) Fact or (B) Opinion

They feed the birds in the park.

Is this a fact or an opinion?

(A) Fact or (B) Opinion

He looks at the toys in the window.

Is this a fact or an opinion?

(**A**) Fact or (**B**) Opinion

Everyone should have a horse.

Is this a fact or an opinion?

(A) Fact or (B) Opinion

The music sounds good.

Is this a fact or an opinion?

(A) Fact or (B) Opinion

She buys a book.

Is this a fact or an opinion?

(A) Fact or **(B)** Opinion

The flowers smell good.

Is this a fact or an opinion?

(A) Fact or (B) Opinion

He must put a stamp
on the letter to mail it.

Is this a fact or an opinion?

(A) Fact or (B) Opinion

Grapes taste better than apples.

Is this a fact or an opinion?

(A) Fact or (B) Opinion

The water feels cold.

Is this a fact or an opinion?

(A) Fact or (B) Opinion

The building is tall.

Is this a fact or an opinion?

(A) Fact or **(B)** Opinion

A. Exercising Your Skill

Do a class survey. Write "Brothers," "Sisters," and "Favorite Food" on the board in three columns. Have each student tell how many brothers and sisters he or she has. Make a tally mark for each answer. Ask students to name their favorite food. List their favorite foods, and tally the answers. Tell which answers are facts and which ones are opinions, and explain why.

B. Expanding Your Skill

Play What's My Job? Think of a job or sport you like. Tell why you like it, but do not tell what it is. Tell facts about it. Have the class guess what job or sport it is.

C. Exploring Language

Write the following sentences on the board. Read the sentences. Write "F" for fact if the sentence tells a fact. Write "O" for opinion if the sentence tells an opinion.

Dogs are the best pets.

Dogs can be big or small.

Cats have sharp claws.

Cats sleep too much.

There is a chickadee in every picture from Unit 1 to Unit 12.

Chickadees are pretty birds.

D. Expressing Yourself

Do one of these activities.

1. Draw a picture of your favorite animal. Tell one fact about the animal. Then tell why it is your favorite animal.

2. Take turns showing your opinion without using words. Examples could be eating a lemon or a hot pepper; smelling a skunk or a rose.

He opens the big gate.

Is this a fact or an opinion?

(**A**) Fact or (**B**) Opinion

Corn grows in a field.

Is this a fact or an opinion?

(**A**) Fact or (**B**) Opinion

The air is cool.

Is this a fact or an opinion?

(A) Fact or (B) Opinion

She climbs the ladder.

Is this a fact or an opinion?

(A) Fact or (B) Opinion

The cows are eating.

Is this a fact or an opinion?

(A) Fact or **(B)** Opinion

Snow is fun.

Is this a fact or an opinion?

(A) Fact or (B) Opinion

The kites fly high.

Is this a fact or an opinion?

(A) Fact or (B) Opinion

The baby **girl** is the best one.

Is this a fact or an opinion?

(**A**) Fact or (**B**) Opinion

Some birds lay big eggs.

Is this a fact or an opinion?

(A) Fact or **(B)** Opinion

Pickles taste good.

Is this a fact or an opinion?

(A) Fact or (B) Opinion

The goat is funny.

Is this a fact or an opinion?

(A) Fact or (B) Opinion

Waking up is fun.

Is this a fact or an opinion?

(A) Fact or (B) Opinion

A. Exercising Your Skill

Take turns finding the bird in each picture from Unit 13 to Unit 24. Tell what the bird is doing. Tell how the bird helps show a fact or an opinion.

B. Expanding Your Skill

Think about your favorite place. Tell a partner two facts about that place. Ask your partner to give his or her opinion of that place. Then tell why it is your favorite place.

C. Exploring Language

Write the following words on the board:

brown   green   hot

red   cool   yellow

Listen to the following sentences. Choose a word from the list on the board that makes sense in the sentence. You can use a word more than once. There are more words than you will need. Then tell me if the sentence is a fact or an opinion.

1. The leaves on the tree are _____.

2. The _____ light means go.

3. A _____ drink is nice on a _____ day.

D. Expressing Yourself

Think about these questions.

1. What do you wear when it is hot outside?

2. What do you wear or carry to walk in the rain?

They will have fun at the zoo.

Is this a fact or an opinion?

(A) Fact or (B) Opinion

Snakes are smooth.

Is this a fact or an opinion?

(A) Fact or (B) Opinion

The alligators are resting.

Is this a fact or an opinion?

(A) Fact or (B) Opinion

The monkeys are chasing each other.

Is this a fact or an opinion?

(A) Fact or (B) Opinion

The peacock is pretty.

Is this a fact or an opinion?

(A) Fact or **(B)** Opinion

Giraffes grow very tall.

Is this a fact or an opinion?

(A) Fact or (B) Opinion

The zebra's stripes
help it hide in the grass.

Is this a fact or an opinion?

(A) Fact or (B) Opinion

The birds have feathers.

Is this a fact or an opinion?

(A) Fact or (B) Opinion

Pandas eat plants.

Is this a fact or an opinion?

(A) Fact or (B) Opinion

The tortoise has a shell.

Is this a fact or an opinion?

(A) Fact or **(B)** Opinion

Fish taste good.

Is this a fact or an opinion?

(A) Fact or (B) Opinion

Lions are big.

Is this a fact or an opinion?

(A) Fact or (B) Opinion

The girl likes the pony.

Is this a fact or an opinion?

(A) Fact or **(B)** Opinion

It is a wonderful day.

Is this a fact or an opinion?

(A) Fact or (B) Opinion

A. Exercising Your Skill

Talk about the people in each picture from Unit 25 to Unit 38. Tell what they are doing. Tell how the people in the picture help show a fact or an opinion.

B. Expanding Your Skill

Take turns acting like your favorite animal. Give one fact about the animal, but do not tell the name of your animal. Ask the other students to guess what animal it is.

C. Exploring Language

Read the following facts about each animal. Have children guess what animal.

I am big and gray. I have a trunk.
I am long and have no legs or feet.
I am tall with long legs and a long neck.
I have a hard shell on my back, and I move very slowly.

D. Expressing Yourself

Choose one of these activities.

1. Play Weather Facts and Opinions. Sit in a large circle with the other students. Choose a person to start. That person tells a fact about weather. The second student gives an opinion about weather. The third student tells a fact, and so on.

2. Think about a storybook or movie you like. Tell a partner three facts about it. Tell your opinion.

Making things with clay is fun.

Is this a fact or an opinion?

(A) Fact or **(B)** Opinion

Scissors are fun to use.

Is this a fact or an opinion?

(A) Fact or (B) Opinion

He reads the book to the class.

Is this a fact or an opinion?

(A) Fact or (B) Opinion

The song sounds good.

Is this a fact or an opinion?

(**A**) Fact or (**B**) Opinion

Soccer is the best sport.

Is this a fact or an opinion?

(A) Fact or (B) Opinion

They hike in the woods.

Is this a fact or an opinion?

(**A**) Fact or (**B**) Opinion

Grandfather gives juice to the team.

Is this a fact or an opinion?

(A) Fact or (B) Opinion

The breeze feels nice.

Is this a fact or an opinion?

(A) Fact or (B) Opinion

She plays checkers with Mother.

Is this a fact or an opinion?

(A) Fact or (B) Opinion

They are eating the bread.

Is this a fact or an opinion?

(**A**) Fact or (**B**) Opinion

She reads to her little brothers.

Is this a fact or an opinion?

(A) Fact or **(B)** Opinion

The dog is wet.

Is this a fact or an opinion?

(A) Fact or (B) Opinion

A. Exercising Your Skill

As a class think of three facts and three opinions about cats. Do the same for another kind of animal.

B. Expanding Your Skill

Play 20 Questions. Choose someone to start by thinking of a person, place, or thing. The other students ask 20 questions to try to figure out what the person is thinking about. The questions can only be answered "Yes" or "No." The student who answers right gets to think of the next person, place, or thing.

C. Exploring Language

Use words from the word list to finish the sentences. Write an "F" if the sentence is a fact. Write an "O" if the sentence is an opinion.

> best   yellow   tall   orange   old

1. The ___ boy could reach the top shelf.
2. The ___ tasted wonderful.
3. The school bus is ___.
4. Mom's cooking is the ___.
5. The ___ cheese smelled bad.

D. Expressing Yourself

Choose one of these activities.

1. Think of a person who is special in your life. Tell a partner three facts about this special person. Tell your opinion about this person.

2. Work with a partner to act out a story. Make up your own story. Use facts and opinions to tell the story.